Fairy stories hold a fascination for children that cannot be equalled. This story has been adapted for beginner readers but if your child is not able to read, you can read this delightful story aloud. For your child, listening to a story in a relaxed atmosphere is a vital part of the learning process. For you, the reader, there is the opportunity to discuss the feelings the story conjures up and the meanings of any unfamiliar words with your child.

Linda Coates Cert Ed, MA.

The Pied Piper of Hamelin

retold by Pat Posner
illustrated by Gill Guile

There was once a little town in Germany called Hamelin. It was a happy, busy town, where the children laughed and played and all the people worked very hard.

Then one day something terrible happened. Hamelin was invaded by rats: big rats, small rats, black rats and brown rats, all with long tails and sharp teeth! The rats stole food, made nests in houses, and even scared away all the cats. The people of Hamelin were very frightened.

They tried chasing the rats with brooms and boarding up the tiny holes in the skirting boards, but still the rats kept coming! A trail of bread crumbs was laid leading the way out of town, but that just made even more rats enter Hamelin. Soon, there were more rats than people!

"We will go to the mayor," decided the people. "It's his job to look after the town so he'll have to think of some way to get rid of the rats." But the mayor couldn't think of anything at all.

The people started to shout angrily at the mayor, and he was frightened. Suddenly, the door of the town hall opened and a strange man, dressed in red and yellow, danced in. He was carrying a whistle pipe. The people stopped shouting at the mayor and gazed at the stranger.

"I am called the Pied Piper," said the man. "I have come to get rid of the rats for you. I can charm any creature to dance away and never come back when I play magic music on my pipe."

The people of Hamelin looked hopefully at the Pied Piper. "Yes," he continued, "I will charm all your rats away and make Hamelin a happy place once more. But you will have to pay me one hundred gold coins."

"If you can rid our town of the rats," shouted the mayor, "we will pay you ten times that amount." The people of Hamelin cheered and stamped in agreement, and the Pied Piper smiled as he looked at them.

The Pied Piper went out into the street and started to play a strange, haunting tune on his pipe. As soon as the rats heard the tune, they came scurrying out from every nook and cranny in the town.

Then the rats began to follow the Pied Piper through the town. They danced behind him, over the hills and through the meadows, enchanted by the haunting music. At last, they came to a deep, wide river.

The Pied Piper sat on the bank of the river and played faster and faster on his whistle pipe. One by one, the bewitched rats jumped into the river. The current was very strong and every single rat was drowned beneath the swirling waters.

When the people of Hamelin awoke the next morning, the rats were nowhere to be found. Hamelin was free! The people ran from house to house, laughing with delight. The celebrations lasted all day long.

Soon, the Pied Piper returned to claim his payment. Why should I pay him? thought the mayor. There is no need now that all the rats have gone. Besides, there is not enough money in the whole of Hamelin to pay what we promised, so I shall just tell him to go.

"You will be sorry for this!" shouted the Pied Piper. "I have rid your town of rats, as I said I would, yet you have broken your promise to pay me. Well, I play more than one tune on my pipe, as you will see."

That very same night, when the moon was full and bright, the Pied Piper began to play the strangest tune. As the music floated over the still, summer air, the children of Hamelin slipped out of their beds. Still half-asleep, they danced into the street below.

The Pied Piper began to dance, too, and beckoned to the children to follow him. Their parents cried out, thinking their children would be drowned just like the rats, but the enchanted children didn't hear their parents as they danced after the Pied Piper and far away.

When he reached the river, the Pied Piper took them along a path that led to a mountain. "He must let them come back now," said the parents. "They can't go any further." However, the Pied Piper played four long notes on his pipe and a doorway in the mountain opened up!

The sound of sweet music, even sweeter than the Pied Piper's, came from inside. Just as dawn was breaking, the children danced into the mountain and when the last child had danced inside, the doorway closed.

All the children were gone. All that is, except for one little boy who was lame and hadn't been able to keep up with the others. "Please wait! Please wait!" he called, but he was too late. The doorway stayed closed.

The little boy sat down and cried, for he had so longed to join his friends in the magic land inside the mountain. Now, there'd be nobody for him to play with. He was the only child left in the whole of Hamelin.

The people of Hamelin were sad, too, for they would no longer hear the sound of laughing children in the streets. "We should have kept our word," said the mayor. "Somehow, we should have paid the Pied Piper for ridding us of the rats."

The mayor sent messengers all over the land to seek the Pied Piper, but no trace of him could be found. Hamelin became quiet, sad and deserted, and the people no longer smiled.

Nothing was ever seen of the children again, though it was said that the sound of their laughter and the Pied Piper's haunting music could sometimes be heard along the path to the mountainside.

The lame boy grew up into a sad and wise man and he vowed that if ever he made a promise, he would always keep his word. He would never forget that somewhere, inside a mountain, his friends danced the years away.